Quiet Time

A GUIDE TO DAILY RENEWAL

Bill Smith

Cover Design: Nancy Carter

Printed in the United States of America

Publisher: Dad, the Family Shepherd
               P.O. Box 21445
               Little Rock, AR 72221
               501-221-1102

TABLE OF CONTENTS

Foreword 3

Introduction 5

Part One: The Appeal of Quiet Time 9

Part Two: The "How To's" of Quiet Time 25

Part Three: Questions and Solutions 37

Time Inventory 43

Addendum: Ideas from Quiet Time Readers 44

Addendum: How Not to Read the Bible 46

Appendix: Quiet Time Resources 47

About the Publisher: Dad, the Family Shepherd 48

"E" (Encouragement) Team Guide 49

Quiet Time Note Pages 57

Quiet Time Material Ordering Information 60

Foreword

I do not know a fruitful Christian man who does not meet the Lord in the morning. I'm sure there are some, I only say that I don't know any.

Note that I say this of men, not women. Many times a woman is directed by circumstances to have her quiet time later in the day, and I know of many who do. Anyone who observed our household when our children were small would know why Lucy had to wait till the older kids were at school and the little ones down for naps to get a decent moment with God. It gave the words "quiet time" a whole new meaning.

But I believe that what a man does before breakfast definitely determines his effectiveness the rest of the day. It is in that morning time with God that his spiritual battle is most often won or lost. Morning Bible reading and prayer shapes the day.

My friend was a general in the British Army. "I tell soldiers," he said, "that if they are under an officer who is not up before 6:00 a.m., they should ask for a transfer."

Hard to get up in the morning? The best solution I know is to form the habit of getting to bed at a reasonable hour each night. Habits can be changed, and new ones formed, with proper motivation. This little book clearly motivates change, and contains many practical pointers on starting your day right.

Consistent, meaningful QUIET TIME is indispensable to a vital walk with God. Bill Smith has written an outstanding guide to coming to know God through the quiet time. His guide rings true because it is rooted in the BIBLE and personal experience. I highly recommend it.

Lorne C. Sanny
Chairman of the U.S. Board
The Navigators

Introduction:
Quiet Time and Homemade Bread

Ours is a noise-wracked society. Pressures from business, family, and the community compete with sales pitches from scores of sources, blaring out to impact our lives.

"Just to get away for awhile" is a commonly heard desire. "A little peace and quiet would do wonders for me; if not for a week, maybe a few days."

Is there a way to "get away" for awhile *every day?*

This book is about a *daily* experience of quiet time, a time alone for spiritual renewal and inner strength. This is how it works in my life (and others I know), and here are some directions for getting started.

Homemade Bread: An Analogy

To begin, an analogy might help. We all like homemade bread. Recently some friends came to our lake house to spend the weekend and brought two loaves. What a surprise! It brought back memories of a time when I baked my own homemade bread on Saturday mornings. It was relaxing (you can really work off some tension pounding dough!), the aroma was great, and friends enjoyed the results (usually).

A quiet time is like homemade bread:

- Directions are provided. This book is one "recipe" for quiet time.

- Baking bread invites innovation. This is a starter; you can build on your own experience. There is no right way to do it, just different ways.

- The results are satisfying to the baker and to those around. Quiet time will become the highlight of your day, and others will recognize the difference in your attitude and personality!

■ Why *homemade* bread?

Breads of all kinds can be bought ready-made at the supermarket. Even fresh baked bread is available. But homemade bread is best by far. No one will argue that. It smells better and tastes better.

You can also buy "prebaked" guides or quiet time books. Some are exceptionally good. But all are second-hand, passing on someone else's experience. This book tells you how to have *your own* personal quiet time *directly from God's Word* itself and feel good about the results.

Read on, and see if your concerns, doubts, or questions are addressed. Then give it a try. The proof is in the eating!

What's Coming? The Format:

Recently in discussing an upcoming meeting, a friend asked, "What is the format?" Since it helps to know where you are going on the front end, here is the way this "how to" book is put together.

FIRST. . . We will cover the benefits and ingredients of quiet time. What is the goal, the purpose? What do you do? How long does it take? What time of day is best? How often? What will make your quiet time a success or a failure? What are the payoffs?

THEN. . . We will talk about the practical "how to's" of a quiet time. These are the "step one, two, and three" directions. These directions encourage your own adaptations, the development of your distinctive "homemade" spiritual bread. Quiet time is a personal experience, not an accomplishment. The enjoyment is in the doing, not just the end result.

> **What will make your quiet time a success or failure?**

FINALLY. . . We will deal with some common questions, such as: "What if I can't understand parts of the Bible?" or "What if I can't get up early enough?" and others.

The Addendum and Appendix sections at the back of this book provide further assistance. In sum, Quiet Time's purpose is to encourage your success.

What quiet time means to me. . .

"The most effective part of my quiet time is for listening. To be silent and listen I have to get beyond myself and my own needs. It's like saying, 'Speak to me rather than listen to me.' I believe it's an essential ingredient for the Holy Spirit to work within our lives."

Tad Krug, President
Ramsey, Krug, Farrell and Lensing
Insurance Agency

Part One:
The Appeal of Quiet Time

A quiet time is a daily period set aside from the world's demands, and our own opinions, to seek refreshment and strength in direct communion with God. It's a time of "God and me" in private.

What is the goal of quiet time? The goal is TO KNOW GOD. It's that simple, and that profound.

It may surprise you that God can be known or that God wants to know you. Let's think about that idea a moment.

That Pesky Question. . .

Have you been with people who, when a name is mentioned, ask, "Do you know them?" The tone is that if you do, you're OK; if you don't, then you're out of it. I call this "interrogative name dropping."

The usual answer is, "Yes, we are friends"; or "I have met them, but do not really know them"; or "No, but I would like to know them." What does it mean to *know* someone?

■ What is involved in knowing?

First, we obviously must *meet* a person in order to get to know them. Then, we must *spend time* with them. The more time we spend together and the more we exchange conversation, the better we get to know them.

To know God, we must first meet him. That is a personal experience. Meeting God is not exactly alike for any two

> **The goal is**
> **TO KNOW GOD.**
> **It's that simple, and that profound.**

people, nor does it lend itself to formulas. Jesus said that meeting God, which he called a "new birth," is like the wind. It blows where it will, and no one can tell where it comes from or where it is going. If you have never met God in this way, consider some introductory aspects.

■ God is Available

The vital truth is that God is available at any time for that first meeting with whomever wants to know him. Jesus Christ settled the sin and separation issue on the cross and in his resurrection. He now says, "Here I am! I stand at the door and knock. If anyone hears my voice, and opens the door, I will come in and eat with him, and he with me," (Revelation 3:20). No appointment is necessary, nor is any special business purpose. God's business is you and me - loving us and making our lives full. We simply need to turn from our own ways (called "sin"), and say "Come in" to Jesus Christ, asking him to take up his residence in our hearts and become our Lord. A relationship is on!

Some people, when we first meet them, create a desire in us to know them better. God is like that. The initial meeting is not the whole experience; it is just the beginning. The question then becomes, "HOW do we get to know him better?" That's the point of quiet time.

■ Get This Straight

God *wants* us to know him. It's staggering to think that the God of the universe could actually *want* to know me, and *want* me to know him, but it's true. He has said so in many ways. The following are just a few:

> "I don't want your sacrifices - I want your love;
> I don't want your offerings - I want you to know
> me."
>
> Hosea 6:6 - *The Living Bible*

The initial meeting is not the whole experience; it is just the beginning.

> "This is what the Lord says: Let not the wise
> man boast of his wisdom or the strong man
> boast of his strength or the rich man boast of
> his riches, but let him who boasts boast about
> this: that he understands and knows me. . ."
>
> Jeremiah 9:23-24a

Jesus Christ, just before his death, prayed to the Father:

> "Now this is eternal life: that they may know
> you, the only true God, and Jesus Christ,
> whom you have sent."
>
> John 17:3

He had told his disciples earlier:

> "I am the good shepherd; I know my sheep
> and my sheep know me - just as the Father
> knows me and I know the Father - and I lay
> down my life for the sheep."
>
> John 10:14

Jesus said of the Holy Spirit:

> "He will bring glory to me by taking from what
> is mine and making it known to you. All that
> belongs to the Father is mine. That is why I
> said the Spirit will take from what is mine and
> make it known to you."
>
> John 16:14-15

This knowledge is personal and experiential, not just intellectual. The kind of knowing in these passages is a process that follows the original meeting, and involves a lifetime of discovery.

God wants us to know him.

Finally, the Bible says:

> "Knowing God results in every other kind of
> understanding."
>
> Proverbs 9:10b - *The Living Bible*

So God wants you and me to know him very well, and that
is the key to every other aspect of life.

The goal of quiet time is simple and clear - to know God
personally. All the suggestions that follow have that as the
objective - to know him.

The Ingredients of Quiet Time

This desire of God to know us on a personal level is
expressed in many ways, but knowing God better is not
automatic. We must devote some effort to knowing him,
just as with anyone. What is needed to make the effort
productive? To find out, let's think about the separate
ingredients of quiet time: Time, the Word of God, the Holy
Spirit, Prayer, and Obedience.

■ Quiet Time Ingredient One: Time

A regular, habitual time every day needs to be devoted to
quiet time. We eat at regular times, and we sleep at
regular times. We can also meet God quietly and personally at a regular time daily.

When? Any time will do, but many find early morning best.
Our minds are more alert, we haven't been subjected to the
pressures of the day, and we are fresh for the day's most
important meeting - with our Creator.

Some find it almost impossible to have quiet time in the
early hours. Other times will do just fine. Throughout
history, however, many have found the first part of the day
ideal for quiet time.

> ***What is needed to make***
> ***the effort productive?***

> "Let the morning bring me word of your
> unfailing love, for I have put my trust in you.
> Show me the way I should go, for to you I lift
> up my soul."
>> Psalm 143:8

> "In the morning, O Lord, you hear my voice; in
> the morning I lay my requests before you and
> wait in expectation."
>> Psalm 5:3

> "He wakens me morning by morning, wakens
> my ear to listen like one being taught."
>> Isaiah 50:4b

Quiet time is high-value time.

> "Better is one day in your courts than a
> thousand elsewhere."
>> Psalm 84:10a

King David, one of the richest and busiest men of his day, considered three years a good swap for one day in God's presence. Certainly a small piece of our day is worth scheduling!

David also made a practice of praising God multiple times throughout his day.

> "Seven times a day I praise you for your
> righteous laws."
>> Psalm 119:164

Daniel, another example, was the appointed administrator of Babylon when the Jews were in captivity. Mighty

Quiet time is high-value time.

Babylon ruled the world. Imagine how hectic Daniel's life was, packed with appointments, duties, and political pressures! Yet we learn that he made a point of pulling aside and going home for prayer three times daily.

> "Now when Daniel learned that the decree had
> been published, he went home to his upstairs
> room where the windows opened toward
> Jerusalem. Three times a day he got down on
> his knees and prayed, giving thanks to his
> God, just as he had done before."
> Daniel 6:10

But morning is best! Morning is a time of wonderful freshness and renewal for the one who waits upon God.

> "I rise before dawn and cry for help; I have put
> my hope in your word."
> Psalm 119:147

Another quiet time observer said:

> ". . . His loving kindness begins afresh each
> day."
> Lamentations 3:23
> *The Living Bible*

We must surrender time to him. How long is not the point; knowing Christ is the objective. Time is immaterial if we are with Christ. He is timeless, and will fill our quiet time and the rest of our lives with his presence.

■ **Quiet Time Ingredient Two: The Word of God**
During our quiet time, we need to *listen* in order to know God. God speaks to us through his Word. We turn to his Word because God thinks differently than we think, and we

Time is immaterial if we are with Christ.

must become acclimated to his way of viewing matters. Notice what Isaiah wrote:

> "'For my thoughts are not your thoughts, neither are your ways my ways,' declares the Lord. 'As the heavens are higher than the earth, so are my ways higher than your ways and my thoughts than your thoughts. As the rain and the snow come down from heaven, and do not return to it without watering the earth and making it bud and flourish, so that it yields seed for the sower and bread for the eater, so is my word that goes out from my mouth: It will not return to me empty, but will accomplish what I desire and achieve the purpose for which I sent it.'"
>
> Isaiah 55:8-11

Jeremiah, another Old Testament believer, said:

> "When your words came, I ate them; they were my joy and my heart's delight, for I bear your name, 0 Lord God Almighty."
>
> Jeremiah 15:16

The value of God's Word is a major theme of the writers of the Bible.

> "I have hidden your word in my heart, that I might not sin against you."
>
> Psalm 119:11

> "The law of his God is in his heart; his feet do not slip."
>
> Psalm 37:31

God thinks differently than we think, and we must become acclimated to his way of viewing matters.

> "The ordinances of the Lord are sure and altogether righteous. They are more precious than gold, than much pure gold."
>
> Psalm 19:9b-10a

Let's compare time every day in God's Word to "much" pure gold. If "much" gold were one ounce per day, then the value would be about $170,000 per year at present prices. Would we take a job at that salary per year to spend time every day in God's Word, assimilating it, "eating" it? Of course! But the Psalmist says that time in God's Word is much more valuable than such a large income; it's a better deal!

Again, the relative value of God's Word and "things" or "gain" is contrasted:

> "Turn my heart toward your statutes and not toward selfish gain. Turn my eyes away from worthless things; preserve my life according to your word."
>
> Psalm 119:36-37

> "I rejoice in following your statutes as one rejoices in great riches."
>
> Psalm 119:14

> "I rejoice in your promise like one who finds great spoil."
>
> Psalm 119:162

The entire 119th Psalm, the longest chapter in the Bible, is about the practical value of God's Word. Each verse says something new about the Word!

God's Word is much more valuable than such a large income; it's a better deal!

The New Testament writers also appreciated the unique qualities of God's Word in our lives.

> "For the word of God is living and active. Sharper than any double-edged sword, it penetrates even to dividing soul and spirit, joints and marrow; it judges the thoughts and attitudes of the heart."
>
> Hebrews 4:12

> "Like newborn babes, long for the pure milk of the word, that by it you may grow in respect to salvation, if you have tasted the kindness of the Lord."
>
> I Peter 2:2-3
> *NASB*

> "So faith comes from hearing, and hearing by the word of Christ."
>
> Romans 10:17
> *NASB*

Finally, Jesus emphasized that God's Word is vital. Both by example and in his teaching, he constantly encouraged attention to the written word.

> "Man does not live on bread alone, but on every word that comes from the mouth of God."
>
> Matthew 4:4

> "You search the scriptures, for you believe they give you eternal life. And the scriptures point to me!"
>
> John 5:39
> *The Living Bible*

"Like newborn babes, long for the pure milk of the word, that by it you may grow. . ."

> "Whoever has my commands and obeys them,
> he is the one who loves me. He who loves me
> will be loved by my Father, and I too will love
> him and show myself to him."
>
> John 14:21

To obey his commands, we must have them; to have them,
we must read, study, and think about them.

Recalling our objective - knowing God - the last part of that
promise is especially powerful in the *Amplified Bible*:

> ". . . and I [too] will love him and will show
> (reveal, manifest) myself to him - I will let
> myself be clearly seen by him and make
> myself real to him."

So, for Jesus Christ to reveal himself to us and be real to
us in our daily lives, the Word of God is central to our quiet
time.

■ Quiet Time Ingredient Three: The Holy Spirit
The Holy Spirit is a mysterious subject, but one work of
God's Spirit is helping us know God personally.

Paul wrote to the Ephesians:

> "I keep asking that the God of our Lord Jesus
> Christ, the glorious Father, may give you the
> Spirit of wisdom and revelation, so that you
> may know him better."
>
> Ephesians 1:17

Jesus talked about the work the Holy Spirit would do after
his resurrection:

> *. . . one work of God's Spirit
> is helping us know God personally.*

> "He will bring glory to me by taking from what is mine and making it known to you. All that belongs to the Father is mine. That is why I said the Spirit will take from what is mine and make it known to you."
>
> John 16:14-15

The Holy Spirit is God in residence in the heart of every believer. He will lead us to a fuller, more personal knowledge of God. Quiet time is a way of allowing the Holy Spirit to deepen our fellowship with the Father.

■ Quiet Time Ingredient Four: Prayer

We *listen* to God talk through his Word. A good relationship, however, is two-way, and God wants to *listen* to us. Our talking to God is called prayer. Does it seem unbelievable that God himself wants to hear from us? Study the following:

> "In the morning, 0 Lord, you hear my voice; in the morning I lay my requests before you and wait in expectation."
>
> Psalm 5:3

> "But when you pray, go into your room, close the door and pray to your Father, who is unseen. Then your Father, who sees what is done in secret, will reward you."
>
> Jesus,
> Matthew 6:6

> "If you, then, though you are evil, know how to give good gifts to your children, how much

The Holy Spirit is God in residence in the heart of every believer.

more will your Father in heaven give good gifts
to those who ask him."

Jesus,
Matthew 7:11

Jesus taught that a special life of "much fruit" is possible.
He gave us the ingredients, which included prayer.

> "If you remain in me and my words remain in
> you, ask whatever you wish, and it will be
> given you. This is to my Father's glory, that
> you bear much fruit, showing yourselves to be
> my disciples."
>
> John 15:7-8

A disciple is a *learner.* Jesus said that his disciples *bear
much fruit as they learn,* thus glorifying the Father. Prayer,
coming out of a life saturated in Christ and his words,
releases this "much fruit."

> "Until now you have not asked for anything in
> my name. Ask and you will receive, and your
> joy will be complete."
>
> John 16:24

It is remarkable that Jesus, who prayed himself, promised
complete and full joy as a result of prayer in his name.
Prayer is joy, not drudgery.

Finally, God's Word says, "You do not have, because you
do not ask God," (James 4:2). Could anything be simpler?
Blessings and answers are just waiting for us. The Father
waits to hear us and respond.

> *Jesus said that his disciples
> bear much fruit as they learn,
> thus glorifying the Father.*

Prayer will naturally lead to expressions of praise and worship, another facet of knowing God.

Prayer is one of the most rewarding aspects of a regular quiet time relationship with Christ.

■ Quiet Time Ingredient Five: Obedience
In quiet time, we will receive leadership from God concerning our lives. As we obey, our knowledge of God increases.

Remember Jesus' words in John 14:21:

> "The person who has my commands and keeps them is the one who [really] loves me, and whoever [really] loves me will be loved by my Father. And I [too] will love him and will show (reveal, manifest) myself to him - I will let myself be clearly seen by him and make myself real to him."
> *The Amplified Bible*

Obedience is also a joyful, free experience. God will not ask us to obey him in any way that will harm us. We are growing children. He will try to stretch us, but will also grow us by asking us to obey him in realistic ways. Don't fear obedience; it is a happy, progressive learning experience. Obedience always leads to new joy and expanded responsibilities.

Obedience usually involves "letting your light shine" kinds of activities. Remember that Jesus taught that men will glorify God when they see the good works done by his followers. Quiet time is not just for personal enrichment. Spiritual growth is meaningless unless shared with others in some way. Obedience is serving the "spiritual loaf" from the oven of quiet time to a world in need of God. The quality of the

> *Obedience always leads to new joy and expanded responsibilities.*

"loaf," as with bread, depends on the care exercised in mixing the ingredients and baking. There simply is no more important activity for man than relating daily to God.

■ The Point of It All

Our quiet time won't get a stamp of approval just because we incorporate these elements. Scheduling time, praying, reading the Bible, or even obedience are not the objectives. They are means by which to reach the objective. Knowing Jesus Christ is the object of quiet time and the only measure of success.

How important is knowing Jesus Christ? Twenty years after his conversion, after all the trials and successes he had experienced, the apostle Paul had refined his life goal:

> "[For my determined purpose is] that I may know him - that I may progressively become more deeply and intimately acquainted with him, perceiving and recognizing and understanding [the wonders of his person] more strongly and more clearly."
>
> Philippians 3:10a
> *The Amplified Bible*

A good quiet time motto is Hebrews 12:2:

> "Let us fix our eyes on Jesus, the author and perfecter of our faith."

Our faith has its origin, not in ourselves, but in Jesus Christ, and what he begins, he finishes!

Knowing Jesus Christ is the object of quiet time and the only measure of success.

A popular hymn by Helen Lemmel expresses this focus:

> "Turn your eyes upon Jesus
> Look full in his wonderful face
> And the things of earth
> Will grow strangely dim
> In the light of his glory and grace."

■ Where Does This Lead?

If you think quiet time is passive and tame, you are in for a surprise! Fellowship with Christ is the heart of the whole matter, and he is active. When we come to KNOW HIM, we naturally want to MAKE HIM KNOWN. Often we get the cart before the horse, wanting to spread the word when we haven't really come to know Christ in a personal way. Serving storebought, second-hand bread is one thing, but serving homemade bread makes a mark! When we speak from our own personal experience, we will see the "much fruit" Christ promised his disciples.

Notice the way Jesus did things:

> "Jesus went up on a mountainside and called
> to him those he wanted, and they came to
> him. He appointed twelve. . . that they might
> be with him and that he might send them out
> to preach. . ."
> Mark 3:13-14

First, he called them to "be with him." Then, from that close association, he sent them out. Sharing Christ and serving others will be natural and enjoyable when we have a daily meeting with him.

As we grow, we are able to help others. Service will become a joyful experience as we get to know the Servant.

> *Fellowship with Christ is the heart of the whole matter, and he is active.*

". . . whoever wants to become great among
you must be your servant, and whoever wants
to be first must be slave of all. For even the
Son of Man did not come to be served, but to
serve, and to give his life as a ransom for
many."

Mark 10:43-45

Quiet time is simply a daily experience with Jesus Christ
from which our whole life draws direction, strength, joy, and
vitality!

Next, the specific "how to's" of quiet time.

What quiet time means to me. . .

*"A personal quiet time with God is as essential to
spiritual health as food is to our physical health.
It is that daily feeding that keeps me in tune and
in touch with God's plan for my life. Reading,
meditating, praying and memorizing make up my
daily menu at dawn."*

Cary H. Humphries
Group Vice President
Cargill Corporation

Part Two:
The "How To's" of Quiet Time

Now that we know the elements and some of the benefits of quiet time, let's get to the specific "how to" steps. Returning to our homemade bread analogy, this is the "mix-one-cup-of-this-with-two-cups-of-that" part of the directions.

Be Careful About Expectations

There are legitimate expectations when you start a quiet time, but also some things you should *not* expect. Unreasonable expectations can undermine any new undertaking. Knowing what to expect reinforces our resolve. What should you expect?

Do not expect a mountaintop experience every time. If you have one, fine. But feelings are deceiving. We live by faith, not feelings. It's true that faith produces feelings, but it is a mistake to depend on or always expect feelings as a payoff.

Do not expect every day to be equal in satisfaction, insight, vitality, or meaning. Each quiet time is fresh and produces its own special lessons and blessings. That's part of the appeal. You'll have so-so days, and also absolutely mind-blowing days. Just like eating, every meal is not a gourmet spread. The ordinary meals are what sustain us and make the gourmet meals recognizable.

Do not expect perfection of yourself in execution of a quiet time. You'll oversleep or miss a day, but don't let that throw you. The object is fellowship with Christ, not a religious ritual. Simply get back with him and continue the next day. Again, like a missed meal, you will find that hunger will drive you to fellowship with him as your spiritual appetite is sharpened and developed.

Expect gradual, persistent growth. We thrive physically on regular, balanced meals. The binges, while stimulating in the short run, leave us feeling bloated and less effective afterward. Spiritually, the most meaningful personal growth is gradual, consistent and progressive. A balanced quiet time diet is likewise very important. These directions will tell how to achieve that balance, including a way to check on your progress. We tend to overlook progress unless we have a means of remembering where we were in the past.

Expect an increasingly satisfying personal relationship with Jesus Christ. The Amplified Bible version of Philippians 3:10 is worth repeating: "(For my determined purpose is) that I may know him - that I may progressively become more deeply and intimately acquainted with him, perceiving and recognizing and understanding (the wonders of his person) more strongly and more clearly." That's the goal of quiet time and should be our expectation!

How to Start

When I used to whip up Saturday morning homemade bread, I first laid out all the ingredients. The same is needed for a quiet time. You will need time, a Bible, a notebook, and a pen. Other helps can be added, but these are the basic ones. Save the additives (seasonings) for later. Let's describe the basics one at a time, and then see how they are put to use.

■ Time

"When?" and "How much?" are the two questions here. "When" is a matter of personal preference and planning. If possible, an early morning hour should be set aside. Our minds and spirits are rested and fresh, we are open to impressions from God's Word and the Holy Spirit, and the day and its opportunities lie ahead of us.

If morning is impossible, then any time during the day or

> ***We tend to overlook progress unless we have a means of remembering where we were in the past.***

night will be fine. The important thing is to have a set time and to develop a habit. When quiet time arrives, you will feel spiritual hunger pangs similar to the physical craving when mealtime rolls around. We are creatures of habit. Runners have an intense desire to exercise when their daily exercise time arrives. Regular activities elicit a signal from our minds. So the important thing is to train ourselves (our hearts) to expect a regular quiet time.

"How long?" is a frequently asked question. The question is necessary because we lead such scheduled lives. But if allowed, "How long?" can subtly undermine the whole purpose of quiet time. An implied "How long do I have to read the Bible and pray to say I've had quiet time?" can creep into our thinking. That attitude is a killer; there are no medals handed out on earth or elsewhere for quiet times. The payoff is a deepening relationship with the living God through his Son, Jesus Christ.

If we had a meeting scheduled with the President of the United States, would we ask, "How long?" Here in Arkansas, the wealthiest man in the United States is down the road. If presented the opportunity, do you think a businessman would ask, "How long do I have to spend meeting with him?" Time with the eternal God is far more desirable in comparison, and time thus spent is invaluable.

The answer to "How long?" has to be worked out by each individual. Daily demands and schedules will dictate part of the answer. If scheduling is critical, start with a small amount of time (say, ten minutes a day) and see what develops. In a nation where an average of four hours a day of television is watched, however, time should not be a problem for most. A positive relationship with Christ will make the question unnecessary, and a more likely senti-

> *The important thing is to have a set time and to develop a habit.*

27

ment will be, "How can I arrange to spend *more* time in solitude with him?"

To return to the homemade bread analogy, a friend has suggested that the amount of time available is like a mixing bowl. Some have a small, ten-minute "bowl;" others have more time, a larger "bowl." The ingredients should be balanced but might vary, given the size of the bowl. Even the smallest bowl should include all the ingredients of the Word, the Holy Spirit, prayer, praise, and obedience. Larger bowls allow more flexibility. Like bread, quiet time can be mixed to taste within a given amount of time.

■ **A Bible**
There are many good study Bibles and systems for Bible reading for quiet time. Some are listed in the appendix of this book, or you can use what you have.

I started with *The One Year Bible*, published by Tyndale House. I heartily recommend it to anyone. Why?

The One Year Bible, as the name implies, leads you through the entire Bible in one year. Most people haven't read the Bible through. Here's your chance, in "bite-sized" pieces every year! And there are a number of other "through the Bible in one year" books and plans.

The One Year Bible is published in several major translations, from *The New International Version* to the Catholic version. So, you can find *The One Year Bible* in the translation you prefer.

The One Year Bible is arranged so that each day's reading includes a brief selection from the Old Testament, the New Testament, the Psalms, and Proverbs. The selections are consecutive from the start within each of the sections; that

Like bread, quiet time can be mixed to taste.

28

is, the Old Testament readings on January 1 start with Genesis, the New Testament with Matthew, etc.

Why is this *One Year Bible* arrangement important?

First, because we are forced to get a "balanced meal" spiritually. We get the whole Bible, not just familiar parts.

A second reason is that comparisons pop up between the Old and New Testaments, and our understanding of God's work over the centuries is enhanced.

A third reason is that our interest is maintained. A constant diet of nothing but your favorite food would be pretty boring; variety is the spice of life. The variety offered in the Bible is incredible, and *The One Year Bible* forces us to "taste" new "dishes" or parts of God's Word we may never read otherwise.

A fourth reason is that the appeal of the Bible is enhanced. The genealogies of the Old Testament may be unappealing to you; they are manageable, however, because each day's reading is brief. You also have the New Testament, Psalms, and Proverbs for that day. Your spiritual plate is like a gourmet meal every day, with a selection that is bound to appeal to your taste in some manner.

A fifth reason is because *The One Year Bible* is laid out so that it is readable. I recommend the paperback edition. It feels like a paperback book and is easier to handle than the hardbound book. So, consider *The One Year Bible* in the paperback edition as your beginning quiet time Bible.

A sixth advantage of *The One Year Bible* is the flexibility it offers. If you decide to start with a small amount of time

> *Your spiritual plate is like a gourmet meal every day, with a selection that is bound to appeal. . .*

daily or if you think the Old Testament is too difficult for you at first, then you can read the New Testament selection only. You will then read through the New Testament in one year. And it is simple to include Proverbs, which is only a verse or two per day. The Psalms reading is brief, too. On average, the entire selection in *The One Year Bible* takes about twenty minutes per day to read straight through with no note taking, and about three-fourths of that is from the Old Testament. This is not to suggest that you neglect the Old Testament, but merely to recognize that, spiritually, we walk before we run. Meditation and note taking are important parts of quiet time and should be included every day, even if it means reading the New Testament only. *The One Year Bible* is a perfect Bible reading "trainer," allowing you to bite off as big a bite as desirable initially and then letting you add to your feast as your appetite naturally increases.

■ The Living Bible

I use *The Living Bible* version of *The One Year Bible* for quiet time. *The Living Bible* is a paraphrase. It is called a "thought-by-thought translation" by Tyndale, the publishers. Words are not translated from the ancient languages so much as thoughts are. Therefore, *The Living Bible* is ideal for devotional reading. Serious study, however, usually calls for a more academically precise translation.

The Living Bible is the most readable version I have found. That opinion must be widely shared, given its popularity. It jumps off the page at you. It reads like a good novel or a personal letter. You will enjoy reading *The Living Bible*. I find myself saying again and again, "I didn't know that was in the Bible!" The passage may be familiar, but the way it is said makes it new and fresh. For example, here is part of

> *. . . recognize that, spiritually, we walk before we run.*

the popular 23rd Psalm in *The Living Bible*:

> "Because the Lord is my Shepherd, I have
> everything I need!"
>> Psalm 23:1
>> *The Living Bible*

However, don't think that you have to buy *The One Year Bible* or *The Living Bible* to start a quiet time. You may use the Bible you have. The important thing is to have a plan. Again, see the appendix for some other good resources.

■ Notebook and Pen
Obtain a notebook about the size of *The One Year Bible* with plenty of good quality paper. Also, keep a pen handy with which you enjoy writing.

Why a notebook, and what do you do with it?

The notebook is a must for quiet time, especially when using *The One Year Bible* instead of a devotional book. You are going to write, in rough form, your own living devotional book as you go along. Before that idea scares you, consider the ways you can use the notebook.

As you read the Bible, jot down thoughts that occur to you. These need not be long. In fact, short statements are better and more easily remembered.

Copy verses that really mean something to you. Why copy Bible verses when the Bible is right there? I have found that the act of copying verses is an excellent form of meditation. I am forced to slow down and concentrate on what I have read, to think through the words. Writing verses is a surprisingly fruitful practice in my own quiet time; try it for yourself.

> *You are going to write, in rough form, your own living devotional book as you go along.*

Meditation is mulling over a passage, thinking about it. Selected verses that really pack a personal punch can also be committed to memory for meditation.

Jot down a "diary" of the previous day's main events, spiritual or otherwise. What would you like to remember five years from now? Jot it down. What has God done in your life that you want to remember as a milestone? Jot it down. I usually have a "yesterday" heading at the beginning of the current day's pages to record memorable events.

Begin each day's pages with the date, the time of day, and the location. You will establish a pattern and, on review days, you will recall situations better.

Be flexible with your notebook. It's yours; no one else will likely see it. (Yet, what a legacy to leave your children someday.) I use white unlined paper and vary my note-taking approach. The quiet time is a living meeting with your Lord. Don't get in a rut. Be responsive to your feelings and inclinations.

Start each day with a brief review of the previous day's notes. This will provide continuity both in the Bible reading and in the lessons you are learning. Another way to use the notebook is to review last year's notes to see what changes may have occurred in your thinking and in your life. We tend to forget and need to remember. The notebook and review is one of the hidden blessings of a vital quiet time.

What to Do and When

You have your Bible, notebook and pen, and your solitude. Now what do you do, and in what order?

> *What has God done in your life that you want to remember as a milestone?*

I'll suggest an order of events with the understanding they are not sacrosanct. A meeting between two persons should go where they want it to go. My quiet times vary, but normally I proceed as follows:

First, I focus my thoughts with a minute of worship and prayer. My favorite prayer is from Psalms: "Open my eyes that I may see wonderful things in your law," (Psalm 119:18). In other words, take the blinders off! For a moment of worship, the words of the hymn are appropriate:

> "When morning gilds the skies,
> My heart awakening cries,
> May Jesus Christ be praised!"

Next, I read *The One Year Bible*, making notes as I go. This is the heart of quiet time and will probably occupy two-thirds of the time spent. As the Holy Spirit helps us, we get to know the mind of God in his Word.

My next step is to pray. The reading of God's Word leads to awareness and confession of faults and needs in our lives. Restitution for any wrongs brought to our mind is important. Once our own life is clear, we can pray for others. This is called intercessory prayer. Intercessory prayer is a service to God, and actually impacts lives and meets needs in others. Some people keep a prayer list and a prayer diary to record the answers as they occur. If that sounds strange to you, be alert in your Bible reading to the teachings on prayer, and implement what you learn in your own way. Your life will be enriched as you discover God's intense interest in you and willingness to meet specific needs in your own life and your friends' lives. James said, "You do not have, because you do not ask God," (James 4:2). Often we do not ask because we neglect to take time

> *Intercessory prayer is a service to God, and actually impacts lives and meets needs in others.*

33

to ask. Quiet time makes that time available. Dedicate part
of it to prayer. What an incredible experience!

Last, I stay alert for opportunities to obey Christ. During
quiet time, we can experience the leadership of God
directly in our lives.

Obedience: The Result That Counts

How does God speak so that we know our orders? This is
a delicate area, one that must be learned. That is why
keeping the Word of God central to quiet time is important.
Our experiences should coincide with God's Word. Also,
subjecting impressions of God's leadership to the test of
time can be important. In all honesty, however, we are
probably overly cautious and sometimes miss the blessing
of obedience through fear of how others might react.

Back to the question: How does God speak? One of the
earliest and clearest indications is from the period right after
the Ten Commandments were given to Israel and the
tabernacle was about to be built from the materials donated
by the people.

God told Moses:

> "You are to receive the offering for me from
> each man whose heart prompts him to give."
> Exodus 25:2b

Here and in other places, the Word indicates that God
speaks to us through our hearts, not our ears. Our hearts
are the center of our beings, and they are equipped to pick
up God's leadings. These leadings are called "promptings"
in the Word.

> *Our experiences should
> coincide with God's Word.*

It has been my experience that I am more spiritually attuned, more in line with God's way of looking at things (because of time in his Word), and more sensitive to his concerns during quiet time. The promptings of my heart are most likely from him. They usually concern someone who needs prayer, or might be hurting and need support. The prompting might concern a particular good work or needed word. Obedience may mean that you invest time with a personal friend, or that you serve Christ by ministering to the sick or the poor. It seems that when God wants something done through one of his children, he puts a strong desire in their heart to do it. These desires should be prayed about and followed! Then, and only then, will we discover the active real-life power and presence of Jesus Christ.

Last. . . Be Persistent

Returning to the analogy of eating regularly, today's quiet time will not carry you for a week or a month. A daily secluded quiet time is necessary for spiritual health, just as regular meals are necessary for maintenance of physical health.

Your quiet time experience will vary; it will have its ups and downs, just like anything. But the overall direction will definitely be up if you start, stay with it, and include all the critical ingredients. Persistence pays.

Next, questions that are common.

What quiet time means to me. . .

"My personal quiet time of praise, confession, supplication and reading the Word has increased my desire and ability to have an intimate relationship with Jesus Christ and to experience the overwhelming love of my heavenly Father."

Lynda Sorrells
Homemaker and Mother

Part Three:
Questions and Solutions

On paper, a quiet time looks appealing and almost automatic. A typical reaction is, "That's just what I need! I'll start right away!" In many cases, a quiet time has been tried before with varying degrees of success and may be on inactive status. Others have never even tried to have a regular quiet time. In either case, the key to success is habitual observation.

What are some of the stumbling blocks to a successful personal quiet time everyday? And how can these difficulties be handled? This list will probably include some you have encountered. Hopefully, the suggestions will be practical and useful.

Nearly all difficulties in establishing a daily quiet time fellowship with Jesus Christ are mental or attitudinal. Few of us do not have access to a Bible, a notebook, and some privacy.

"What if I don't have time?"

This is the most common reaction to the desire of Christ for part of our day alone with him. The way to deal with it is to recognize a couple of facts.

We all have exactly the same amount of time every day - twenty-four hours. How we utilize that time is the only difference. A "time inventory" is included in the back of this booklet to help you understand how you are using your allotted time. Fill out your own time inventory. You can then make a deliberate choice to give the daily meeting with Jesus Christ high priority.

Second, there is always enough time to do God's will. David said "My times are in your hands," (Psalm 31:15) and that is true of every person. Acknowledge God's ownership of time, so he can bless all your times.

"What if I can't get up early? I'm not a morning person."

Fine. Establish your daily quiet time in the evening or at some other time during the day, and be there at the appointed hour. Some Christians have their quiet time just before retiring. You could pray about your sleeping habits and morning attitude. I know people who have asked God in prayer to help them awaken early and be fresh for a meeting with him, and have found that the ability to "rise and shine" becomes theirs!

Remember, though, that there are twenty-four hours every day; don't let a particular preference stand in the way. God is on watch around the clock, and he is able to meet you at your convenience. Remember David, Daniel and the other busy people who met God daily at regular hours.

"What if the Bible confuses me?"

You're not alone. Questions arise daily from my lack of understanding. Adopt the attitude that you will pick up truths and directions that you do understand and can act on, and leave the matters that are beyond your understanding for future discovery. After all, we are disciples, which means learners. We will remain disciples and never will learn it all. God is larger than the combined ability of all mankind to comprehend. So, be like a treasure hunter. Don't get hung up on academic or intellectual questions; rather, be on the lookout for your own spiritual treasures that you can discover and use.

The desire to understand and know God's Word better will be a natural outgrowth of quiet time. Deeper study can be

---

What quiet time means to me. . .

"Quiet time provides that most necessary daily focus on the Lord, a time of knowing he is more than adequate in all things."

> *James Strawn III*
> *Chairman and CEO*
> *Electronic Imaging Services, Inc.*

aided by various helpful sources. Reading the Bible through every year with *The One Year Bible* will also contribute to understanding. However, Bible study on a more academic or informational basis should be done outside the quiet time. During quiet time, keep the focus on being open to the Holy Spirit's prodding and teaching in practical, life-changing ways.

"What if I have no privacy?"

This is occasionally true in the home, especially if the family is large and demands are many. Some solve this problem by arising early, while everyone else is sleeping. Others have their quiet time in their office or even in their car. Jesus advised going into your closet, shutting the door, and praying. Privacy can be found.

"What if I think about God during the day, even praying on and off? Won't that be enough?"

Such attitudes and practices are commendable, and are even encouraged in the Word of God. We are told to "pray always." Meditation is also encouraged. However, there is something uniquely beneficial for growth in drawing aside for a time of concentrated attention to the living Christ, to his Word, and to prayer. He is worthy of our full attention for a time every day. You will find that a daily quiet time will only enrich the rest of your spiritual life during the day.

"I don't like to be legalistic in my Christian life, to have a checklist. I like to let it flow and be free."

What quiet time means to me. . .

"A friend told me, 'Jim, you must approach God slowly on your knees.' That is surely the essence of our relationship to our Lord."

**Dr. Jim English
Physician and Surgeon**

There is merit in the attitude of freedom in Christ, and quiet time is certainly not mandatory for anyone. And it is not a way to gain favor with God! In fact, God doesn't need it at all - we do. As we need to eat, sleep, and exercise, so we need daily spiritual nourishment and exercise. Quiet time is simply a disciplined way to try to keep our "spiritual freedom" muscles toned up and in good shape. Our freedom in Christ will mean more as a result of disciplined exposure to him and his Word.

Discipline is one of the outgrowths of the Christian life. In fact, the words "discipline" and "disciple" come from the same root. As the Holy Spirit invades our lives progressively through quiet time, we will realize what Paul meant:

> "But the fruit of the Spirit is love, joy, peace, patience, kindness, goodness, faithfulness, gentleness and self-control (discipline)."
> Galatians 5:22-23a

Conclusion

When facing these and other questions, submit them to the Lord himself and bring them under the realm of his influence by faith. Jesus Christ lives and is more than willing and able to "disciple" us as he did his early followers.

> "Now to him who is able to do immeasurably more than all we ask or imagine, according to his power that is at work within us. . ."
> Ephesians 3:20

What quiet time means to me. . .

"Quiet Time is the way I recharge my batteries for the day's events. I need daily power from Christ to stay charged."

Rowland Smith
Investment Manager

Finally. . .

Get started. Use your present Bible, or obtain a *One Year Bible*. Acquire a special notebook for quiet time (starter note pages are included at the conclusion of this book).

Begin tomorrow in *The One Year Bible* or with your selected reading schedule. Follow the suggestions in "Part Two: The 'How To's' of Quiet Time." Glean truths from your reading and note them. Think about the passages and their application for you. Above all, make quiet time a period of worship of the living Lord. Listen to his Word, wait on his directions, allow him to speak to your heart in silence. Focus on him.

Then, pray and commit to God the many needs in your life. "Turn them over. . ." Trust him. Hold others up to him in prayer, being confident of his intervention.

From worship, meditation on the Word of God, and prayer will come the quiet assurance of his presence. The day ahead will then be directed, fruitful, and more joyful.

You have started your day with God, the source of all life!

"[For my determined purpose is] that I may know him - that I may progressively become more deeply and intimately acquainted with him, perceiving and recognizing and understanding [the wonders of his person] more strongly and more clearly."
   Philippians 3:10a - *The Amplified Bible*

What quiet time means to me...

"I discovered the value of having a daily quiet time while a midshipman at the U. S. Naval Academy at Annapolis. God used it to change my life and give me the spiritual foundation on which to build my life."
   Hal Guffey, Chairman of the Board Emeritus International Students Inc.

Time Inventory

Evaluate the time spent daily doing the following and decide on a manageable quiet time allotment. Start with a short period of time; that will leave you hungry for more. You can always increase quiet time, but don't try to bite off too much in the beginning. Be encouraged by success, and then your desire will grow.

ACTIVITY	HOURS
Working	_____
Recreational Activities	_____
Reading Newspapers	_____
Watching TV	_____
Quiet Time	_____
Sleeping	_____
Eating	_____
Personal Care	_____
Reading Magazines	_____
Driving To and From Work	_____
Other:	_____

My daily quiet time will be about _____ minutes, normally at _____ (the time of day).

Dated: _____

Addendum:
Ideas from Quiet Time Readers

- Find a quiet time friend. Once a week, share newly discovered verses, prayer needs, and insights. Encourage each other in your quiet time and Christian walk.

- A husband and wife each use *The One Year Bible* for their daily quiet time. Upon retiring at night, they share their favorite verse from that day's reading and briefly discuss it. Then they take turns ending the day with a word of prayer.

- A group of friends all use *The One Year Bible* for quiet time. When they get together socially, they often find themselves discussing what they have read that day or the past week, and the application of what they have read.

- A nationally prominent consulting firm meets daily, reads *The One Year Bible* selection, and prays as part of their business day.

- Two businessmen who live across the country from each other talk monthly by long distance to compare quiet time notes and encourage each other in living out what they are learning.

- Many people send a copy of Quiet Time to friends or associates. Some attach a note of encouragement with a word about what the practice has meant to them.

- Receive the *Quiet Time* newsletter for ongoing encouragement, ideas, and insights from others. Send the newsletter to friends as a gift. Write *Quiet Time*, P.O. Box 8702, Little Rock, Arkansas 72217 for a sample copy.

- Write to the above address and offer your experiences and insights to the *Quiet Time* newsletter for possible sharing with others.

Addendum:
How Not to Read the Bible

These two methods of Bible reading are tried by everyone sooner or later. They are both doomed to fail as quiet time practices, so we are describing them in an effort to encourage more fruitful approaches. The two are *The Novel Approach* and *The Sandbox Method*.

The Novel Approach

"I've always wanted to read the Bible through, so I'm going to start at Genesis and read straight through to the end," says the new enthusiast. We all try this because we think of the Bible as one book, like a "novel." It is actually a whole library of very different books, written centuries apart, that are linked by one cohesive theme or story. Also, the books are not arranged chronologically in the Bible. One of the recommended study Bibles or aids in the "Quiet Time Resources Appendix" will help you understand these aspects of the Bible.

Do not try this. You'll reach Leviticus and Numbers, which are the law books, and get bogged down. The balanced approaches recommended in Quiet Time work. Make it easy on yourself and start with a balanced method that is likely to succeed.

The Sandbox (or "Random") Approach

Did you ever watch young children in a sandbox? They reach for this toy and that toy, build this mound and then that house. They have a ball! The Sandbox Approach is one way to handle the Bible and, in fact, is occasionally good. But it will NOT do for habitual spiritual feeding and growth!

"I just open my Bible at random and start reading," says the Sandbox Christian. I'm not knocking this, because it is a "no-agenda" way to "delight" in God's Word. Recalling random verses you've underlined, finding notes on the margin of your Bible, or discovering new passages in this way can be invigorating.

But for consistent growth through fellowship with Jesus Christ, a more regular, disciplined agenda is preferable. Go with proven approaches instead of quick-and-easy intuitive methods. Balanced discipline pays great dividends!

Appendix: Quiet Time Resources

This list includes recommended helps with which the author is familiar. Check with a Christian bookstore or contact as indicated.

Bible Paraphrases and Translations:
The One Year Bible, (various editions) Tyndale House
The Amplified Bible, Zondervan Publishing House

Study Bibles:
The NIV Study Bible, Zondervan Publishing House
The Ryrie Study Bible, Moody Press
The Life Application Bible, Tyndale House Publishers

Bible Study Aids:
What The Bible Is All About, Mears, Tyndale House
Halley's Bible Handbook, Zondervan Publishing House
Explore The Bible Yourself, Navpress*

Quiet Time Aids:
"Daily Walk, A Guide Through The Bible in One Year"**
"Closer Walk, A Guide Through The New Testament in One
    Year"**
Seven Minutes With God, Navpress*
Appointment With God, Navpress*

Scripture Memory and Meditation:
Growing In Christ, Navpress*
The Topical Memory System, Navpress*

Other Books and Booklets:
The Inner Life, Andrew Murray (various publishers)
Taking Men Alive, Charles H. Trumbull, Revell

*Navpress books are available through most Christian bookstores or
  directly from Navpress, Box 6000, Colorado Springs, CO 80934
  (1-800-366-7788).

**Available from Walk Through the Bible (1-800-554-9300) or the
  Navigators, Colorado Springs, Colorado (1-800-228-2098).

About The Publisher

Tom Landry, former coach of the Dallas Cowboys: "I have followed Dave Simmons and his ministry since he left the Dallas Cowboys and believe he has the message and the heart to effectively equip men to be stronger family shepherds."

Dave Simmons, Dallas Cowboy linebacker, didn't dream that he would someday start Dad, the Family Shepherd to help men implement God's method of family leadership. While playing pro football, however, he laid a foundation by attending seminary to prepare for full-time Christian service.

After retiring from football, he and his wife, Sandy, founded a camping ministry called King's Arrow Ranch where, for twenty years, they worked with youth. They saw kids' lives changed, but realized that the catalyst for permanent correction lay in the home.

In the meantime, Dave and Sandy expanded their outreach by speaking to Campus Crusade Family Life Conferences around the world.

Dave's conviction that the father is the leader (shepherd) of the family, and his own experiences as a father, led him to develop the curriculum for his weekend conference called "Build Your House on the Rock." Thousands of men nationwide have heard Dave's thrilling presentation and benefited by participating in this conference and the related "E" (Encouragement) Teams.

About sixteen major conferences are conducted annually under the sponsorship of churches and Christian groups. Video conferences minister to smaller churches or groups. Through the conferences, books, articles and their own newsletter, Dad, the Family Shepherd is meeting a vital, growing need for today's fathers.

Quiet Time is one of a select group of books chosen by Dad, the Family Shepherd for the Shepherd's Bookshelf series to help build men and their families. For more information on Dad, the Family Shepherd ministries, write Dad, the Family Shepherd, P.O. Box 21445, Little Rock, AR 72221.

"E" (Encouragement) Team Guide

Dad, The Family Shepherd's conference ministry fosters "E" Teams of four or five men who meet regularly to encourage one another in faith and fatherhood. Several "E" Team guides from the ministry focus the Team's attention on specific areas. Quiet Time can be used as an "E" Team Course with the objective of establishing and/or improving a man's daily walk with God, thereby equipping him to be a better father.

Small groups of all types can use the guide. Simply make minor adjustments in terminology.

The guide which follows features a series of questions that naturally lead the discussion into areas of need and action. There are several ways to use this "E" Team Guide:

1. Team members can write out answers to each question on the assigned section for the coming week. Then members can read and discuss their answers In the meeting.

2. A less fruitful approach, but a viable one, is to read each question and discuss it in the group meeting without the early preparation. Of course, this assumes that each team member has studied the appropriate section of the Quiet Time book before the meeting.

3. The guide can be used one-on-one in discipleship training or as a quiet time refresher. However, groups of four or five should provide the most effective and dynamic setting.

4. The guide is keyed to the material in the Quiet Time book by titled section, so that any amount of material may be covered for the next "E" Team meeting; each team can move at its own pace. Four or five sessions are normally sufficient to cover the material in an "E" Team setting.

5. Group discussion and sharing are more important than the "right" answer. Groups can develop principles of their own and follow lines of thought within the broad scope of the subject. However, discussion that "chases rabbits" or gets away from a biblically-based focus should be discouraged. The most fruitful endeavor will apply God's Word to daily life.

"E" Team Study Guide Questions

"The best model of fatherhood for our children is our own relationship with God the Father," Anon.

■ Introduction: Homemade Bread

1. What common motivation for quiet time does the author mention in the introduction?

2. What do you do to "get away from it all" daily other than quiet time? How does that activity affect your life?

3. What point does the author make in the homemade bread analogy?

4. Briefly share your own experience in the past with having a quiet time. What was excellent? What were points that could use improvement?

5. Write a goal statement for this study, stating what you want as a result, and share it with your "E" Team.

■ Part One: The Appeal of Quiet Time
Knowing God

1. What are the steps involved in knowing someone? (Three are mentioned in Quiet Time.)

2. Briefly describe one of your best friendships, how you met and why you enjoy your friend's company.

3. How did Jesus Christ define eternal life in John 17:3?

4. Describe to your "E" Team how knowing God might differ from knowing a physical friend.

5. List in your own words several benefits you believe would come to you from knowing God well over the years.

6. Share with your "E" Team your own experience of coming to know Christ personally the first time.

7. Relate in a few sentences your thoughts reading the Bible in a "listening" mode daily. What are the problems? What is the payoff?

8. Describe to the group your number one desire relative to prayer as Father power; what do you want for your children out of your prayer life?

9. How would you go about receiving "to do" obedience orders from God? Make a commitment to do that this week; share the results next meeting.

Quiet Time Ingredient One: Time

1. List and prioritize, in your own opinion, four or five essential components of a vital daily time with God.

2. Tell your group why you chose your top priority item.

3. Report to your "E" Team the approximate amount of time (be honest) you spend daily:
   Watching TV_____
   Watching TV commercials_____
   Reading newspapers_____
   Reading magazines_____
   On your job_____

4. Now think, and tell the group, the approximate amount of daily time you spend:
   Listening to your children, really listening_____
   In focused conversation with your wife_____

Focused listening, talking, and praying to God when alone_____(meditating on his Word)

5. Compare answers to questions 3 and 4. Are there any changes you would like to make? How can you make them? Relate to your "E" Team what these are, and ask for accountability checking over a specified period of time (one week or one month, don't go too long).

Quiet Time Ingredient Two: The Word of God

1. What appeals to you most about the Bible? Why?

2. What is your favorite Bible verse or passage?

3. What can be a source of joy to us according to Jeremiah 15:16?

4. What does Psalm 119:14 mean in your life?

5. What is the greatest evidence that God can and does act in men's lives according to John 14:21?

Quiet Time Ingredient Three: The Holy Spirit

1. Where does the Holy Spirit live?

2. What is one work of the Holy Spirit according to Jesus in John 16:14-15?

3. What can you do to get the Holy Spirit's help in making your quiet time vital and real? What is your part? What is his part?

Quiet Time Ingredient Four: Prayer

1. What would be different about your wife's life if you prayed for her every day?

2. Choose one scriptural command relative to children and pray that for your children for one week. Share your experience the next "E" Team meeting.

3. Visualize fatherhood (or your own father): what one activity do you recall that was most godly in influence? What one godly activity will your children most likely recall about you in twenty years?

4. Brainstorm with your "E" Team practical ideas for daily prayer with your wife, other than a blessing at your meals.

5. Brainstorm practical ways to take the lead in praying with your children habitually.

Quiet Time Ingredient Five: Obedience

1. How does a daily quiet time with God enrich your life? Relate one way to your "E" Team.

2. How does the answer to #1 involve obeying God in serving others in your sphere of influence?

3. Think of obeying God. Share with the group what you most fear when you think of obedience to God. Now share your most honest expectation of what obedience means. What does God's promise in John 14:21 mean (put it in your words)?

4. Note during the coming week one prompting and "obedience" to God's Word which arose out of quiet time. Report to your "E" Team what happened and how the other person(s) responded (this should be light and natural, not heavy or mysterious).

Summary: The Point of It All

1. What was the Apostle Paul's goal after 20 years of service to Christ according to Ephesians 3:20 in the *Amplified Bible*? Restate it in your own words, bottom line.

2. What is the focus of having a consistent quiet time?

3. Tell your "E" Team one way that goal would impact

your:
    Personal life_____
    Home life_____
    Business life_____

■ Part Two: The "How To's" of Quiet Time

1 . Review the five "expectations" on pages 25-26 of the
Quiet Time book. What positive expectation most
appeals to you? Why? What "do not" most applies to
you? Why? (Choose one of the two on pages 25-26,
or state your own expectation.)

2. Tell your "E" Team "when" you plan to have your quiet
time. What are the advantages (disadvantages) of that
time? Report in confidence "how long" you usually
take for your quiet time with Christ.

3. Explain the Bible version or type you use and why you
like it. This may point others in your group to needed
help.

4. Organize a spiritual notebook for your quiet time.
What sections did you include? Why? If you have a
notebook already, report to your "E" Team how you
use it.

5. Discuss the "legacy" you hope to leave your children
(land, savings, stocks, or house etc.). What tangible
evidence of your walk with God will they find? How
could a quiet time notebook fit into your "legacy" plans?

6. Describe one experience in your life where persistence
made the difference between success and failure.
What does persistence mean in terms of a quiet time?
What steps will help you be confident of success?

■ Part Three: Questions and Solutions

1. From the author's list of questions (pages 37-39),
which one is most applicable to you? Relate to your
"E" Team why you chose this question and hash out a
solution. (Of course, state your own question if the
author's doesn't "fit.")

2. Describe your perception of discipline in football. How is it practiced? Taught? What is a disciple? Relate your answers to a daily "huddle" (quiet time) with Christ.

3. According to Galatians 5:22-23, who is the Christian's ultimate source of discipline, the Christian's "coach?"

■ Final Session: Quiet Time Wrap-up

1. Report to your "E" Team your confidential answers to the Time Inventory on page 43.

2. Choose one idea from page 44 and do it. Report the results to your "E" Team.

3. Review the "Resources" on page 47 as a team. Encourage broader knowledge of and use of resources by loaning a team member a resource you have found useful.

4. Final play: Select one member of your "E" Team as a quiet time teammate for one month. Use the "Playsheet" provided. Set a time for a weekly phone "check-in" to see how things are going. Rotate leadership responsibility for these phone meetings. During the "check-in," report how you are doing in your quiet time commitment, what you are doing during your quiet times and the practical, positive results you are experiencing. Also, discuss any problem areas. Pray for each other daily and at the conclusion of your weekly phone meeting. A REMINDER: Start small, be hungry for more. You might commit to one, two or three quiet times the first week, and then add more each week. Aim for PROGRESSION, not perfection. Execute this final play for one month.

QUIET TIME ASSIGNMENT

Step 1 Team up with a quiet time partner:

Name _____

Phone _____

Step 2 Take a minute and discuss the focus verse; share with your partner the single most important truth that you derived from this verse; or share a verse from one of your quiet times.

> "[For my determined purpose is] that I may know him - that I may progressively become more deeply and intimately acquainted with him, perceiving and recognizing and understanding [the wonders of his person] more strongly and more clearly."
>
> Philippians 3:10a - *The Amplified Bible*

Step 3 Set a time for your "check-up" call and one partner assume leadership next week. Will rotate for four weeks:

Day _____

Time _____

Phone # _____

Expect to come to "know him" progressively.

QUIET TIME NOTES

Date_____ Day_____ Time_____

Place_____

"Teach me, 0 Lord, to follow your decrees..."
Psalm 119:33

QUIET TIME NOTES

Date _____ **Day** _____ **Time** _____

Place _____

"*Let me understand the teaching of your precepts. . .*"
Psalm 119:27

QUIET TIME NOTES

Date _____ **Day** _____ **Time** _____

Place _____

"*I run in the path of your commands,
for you have set my heart free.*"
Psalm 119:32

The Quiet Time Newsletter

If you would like a FREE sample copy of the quarterly *Quiet Time Newsletter*, write the address below or phone toll-free.

Topics include: improving your quiet time with ideas from others in many walks of life, tips on finding time in your day to maintain a quiet time, quotes from Christian classics, suggestions for building your Christian life, reviews of new resources and ideas and many other topics.

The goal of the *Quiet Time Newsletter* is to encourage you in your personal quiet time experience.

Quiet Time for Friends

Since the day Quiet Time was written and shared privately, readers have requested copies for gifts to family, friends, business associates, and others. CEOs of corporations have given it to all management level personnel. University leaders have forwarded it to faculty members. Others have used it as the basis of Bible study groups or Sunday school classes.

Because of this, Quiet Time is made available at $2.00 each if ordered in volumes of ten or more.

If you have enjoyed Quiet Time, pass it on to others. . .

To order, call or write:

Dad, The Family Shepherd
P.O. Box 21445
Little Rock, AR 72221
1-800-234-DADS

Others on <u>Quiet Time</u>. . .

"Bill Smith has combined business pragmatism with spiritual insight to produce the booklet, <u>Quiet Time</u>. It's easy to read and understand, profound in its admonition, and scriptural in its basis of proof. I recommend it highly to Christian businessmen to share with others in the workplace."

> *Cary H. Humphries*
> *Group Vice President*
> *Cargill Corporation*

"The <u>Quiet Time</u> guide has helped to focus my special morning times with God and has likewise helped those with whom I have shared this treasure."

> *Dr. James Young, Chancellor*
> *The University of Arkansas at Little Rock*

"<u>Quiet Time</u> is a step by step guide to every new Christian on how to develop a practical and powerful devotional life centered in the Word of God. It will serve as a dynamic refresher course for experienced Christians. My thanks to Bill Smith for his resourcefulness in putting this excellent guide together."

> *Dr. Hal W. Guffey*
> *Chairman of the Board Emeritus*
> *International Students, Inc.*

"No man can keep a right perspective on life without consistent daily 'check-ins' with God. A daily quiet time is a must in order to keep properly oriented. This manual offers a common sense approach. It shows how to put organization and structure into your quiet time and yet allows for plenty of personal freedom. This is the finest quiet time manual of its kind I have seen."

> *Dave Simmons*
> *Founder and Director*
> *Dad, The Family Shepherd*

Bill Smith is an investment advisor with broad business experience that ranges from IBM computer marketing to agriculture, real estate and investment banking.

He began his investment career in 1971 with Stephens Inc., a private Little Rock investment banking firm. He traveled the world advising leading international money managers on U.S. investments and also directed the firm's capital management division. In 1984, he founded his own investment management firm, Smith-Hines Inc., in Little Rock, Arkansas, where he resides.

Quiet Time was written in 1987-88 and reproduced several times privately in response to a growing number of requests. Dad, The Family Shepherd, a national conference ministry for fathers, selected Quiet Time as part of its Shepherd's Bookshelf series and published this edition.

Smith says, "I am gratified by the response to Quiet Time. Apparently, others have the same needs and desires I have come to recognize. I am especially glad to have Dad, The Family Shepherd select the book for their Shepherd's Bookshelf. I know of no ministry with a more vital and timely focus than Dave Simmons' conference outreach. Through DFS, men have a way to learn how to be effective family leaders and fathers. I am hopeful that many others will come to value a daily quiet time with Christ through the simple suggestions found in this book."